The Soul

in Paraphrase:

Poetry as Prayer

The Soul in Paraphrase:

Poetry as Prayer

Edited and Introduced

by James Green

Resources for a Poetry Retreat

by Sheryl O'Sullivan

Bridges of Ross Books

Macon, Georgia
USA

Ross, County Clare
Ireland

The Soul in Paraphrase: Poetry as Prayer

Copyright ©2016 by James E. Green
All Rights Reserved

Cover design: James E. Green

Bridges of Ross Books

2720 Riverside Drive #7435
Macon, Georgia 31209-7435

Ross, Kilbaha,
Kilrush, County Clare
Ireland

The Library of Congress Cataloging-in-Publication Data

Green, James E.

The Soul in Paraphrase: Poetry as Prayer

      p. cm.

      Includes bibliographical references.

        ISBN 978-0-9961164-1-1

        1. Poetry. 2. Prayer. I. Title.

        2016

Printed in the United States of America

*The very essence of our life as conscious beings,
all day and every day, consists of something
which cannot be communicated except by hints,
similes, metaphors . . .*

C.S. Lewis, in "The Language of Religion"

*A poet's affair is with God, to whom he is
accountable, and of whom is his reward.*

Robert Browning, in a letter to John Ruskin

All poetry is prayer.

Samuel Beckett, in a review of the poet Thomas MacGreevy

Acknowledgments

The poems that appear in this anthology are in the public domain. The editor and publisher gratefully acknowledge the many previous publishers from decades and centuries past. Although the editor and publisher have made every effort to determine that these poems are, in fact, in the public domain, they will be pleased to correct any error brought to their attention by requesting appropriate permission.

Table of Contents

Extension Activities

Scripture References
Reflections
Discussion Questions
Suggested Activities
Ritual and Prayer
Extension Activities

Scripture References
Reflections
Discussion Questions
Suggested Activities
Ritual and Prayer
Extension Activities

Introduction:

Poetry as Prayer

When is a poem a prayer? At first it seems like a matter of simple deduction: Writing is hard work, and St. Benedict tells us that work is prayer. Therefore, we might conclude, as Samuel Beckett did, that "All poetry is prayer." However, we know logically, despite these assurances, that not all poetry is prayer because we know that not all work is prayerful. There must be some quality in work making it prayerful. If we examine the many kinds of work, eventually we see that the type of work has nothing to do with its prayerfulness. Benedict considered cleaning stalls in a stable a potentially prayerful vocation, just as prayerful as milking the cows or illuminating the Gospels. What makes work prayerful has something to do with the purpose the worker gives to the work and whether the work engages the worker in dialogue with God. The question of when a poem is also a prayer is really two questions: First, what is poetry and, second, what is prayer?

When poetry achieves the distinction of art, it has its own intrinsic value. Whatever utility we give to it does not add to or diminish it as art. So, when we say poetry can be a prayer or it can help us to pray, we need to recognize we ourselves as giving the poem this quality. In his famous "Ars Poetica," Archibald MacLeish writes that "A poem must not mean but be." Similarly, Wallace Stevens writes, ". . . a poem is not about the thing; it is the thing." The poem must be appreciated for what it is—a work of art. And, we must resist the temptation to define poetry as something it does not have to be in order to be valued as art. In other words, a poem is not necessarily a prayer. Even so, we can read some poems and know, because of what they say to us, that they are prayers. The voice in the poem is speaking to God, or God is speaking to us through the poem. Sometimes that voice is quietly contemplative, as in

Mary Oliver's "The Blackwater Woods," and other times it is ecstatic, such as Gerard Manley Hopkins' "God's Grandeur." The voice might be grateful, or it might be confused. It might even be angry. But always, when a poem is a prayer, the voice in the poem is seeking to be in the presence of God—to speak with and listen to God.

We also know some prayers are poems merely by the way they are written or spoken. When a prayer is also a poem, it uses metaphor to communicate a spiritual experience the poet and the reader (or listener) share. In *The Poetics*, Aristotle writes that the poet "must have command of metaphor" and "to make good metaphors implies an eye for resemblances." Metaphor is the medium between what a reader knows or feels and a deeper, richer understanding of that reality. For example, in the "Twenty Third Psalm," when the psalmist compares God to a shepherd and relief from the stress of daily life to "green pastures" and "still waters," the listeners, who were steeped in a pastoral culture, identified personally with the psalmist's sense of calm and protection because both the listeners and the psalmist understood the function of the shepherd and felt the calming presence of God.

When we consider poetry and prayer separately, we find each has qualities in common. A good poem finds expression for a particular experience shared by both the poet and the reader, and then it condenses that experience so that both the reader and the poet find themselves together, both sharing the same feeling and absorbing the same spirit at the very tap root of that experience. As Emily Dickinson writes, a poem becomes transformational when it "Distills amazing sense / From ordinary meanings."

Prayer is also transformational. In prayer we seek to communicate with God. Whether formal or informal, elegant or simple, prayer is the door we open to meet and nurture our relationship with God. Prayer can be either conversational or lyrical. Prayer can occur as liturgy in a church or in a state of silent awe during a walk along the beach at sunrise. Whatever manner we choose or wherever we happen to be when we are at prayer matters not. However, what does matter is the desire to be with God.

When we read the poems of Emily Dickinson, we witness this desire by joining her lifelong conversation with God. Of course, her prayers are as unorthodox as her poems. In "Where Thou Art—That—Is Home," she asks no questions, draws no conclusions, makes no petitions. She merely expresses her joy of being "at home" with God the way one might speak of a close friend. For her, "Home" is not a location ("I scarce esteem Location's Name"); it is wherever she meets God in prayer.

When we read the poems of Thomas Merton, we share the stillness of his contemplative life as a Trappist monk while he listens for God—as he attempts to "Disappear into God." In "Night Flowering Cactus," we and the night flowering cactus disappear into the mysterious darkness of the night before we can flower. The poem can be read as a spiritual autobiography of Merton, and it helps to remind us of the conditions necessary for spiritual growth.

The contemplative tone in Merton's poems is found also in the poetry of Denise Levertov, whose explanation of the poet's vocation is unmistakably connected to prayer. In *The Poet in the World*, she writes, "So—as the poet stands open-mouthed in the temple of life, contemplating his experience, there comes to him in the first words of the poem: the words which are to be his way into the poem, if there is to be a poem." We easily adapt Levertov's words to prayer, and when we read her poems we share her attention to God's creation through metaphors drawn from nature.

Reading a poem of prayer is, like the reading of any poem, as much a matter of *disposition* as it is of *method*. Of course, there are techniques for reading poetry—explication of a poem can and often does become nothing less than arcane. But it is the reader's attitude—an openness to new perspectives, an appreciation for inventive language, and a willingness to engage with symbol and think imaginatively—that is the connective tissue to a poem's being. Matthew Arnold, in one of his *Essays on Criticism*, writes, "more and more mankind will discover that we have to turn to poetry to interpret life for us, to console us, to sustain us." The reader of poetry must approach a poem believing that the experience will have the power to interpret, and console, and sustain, just as does the experience of prayer.

Still, there is *some* method to reading poetry as prayer. Of course, hardly anyone agrees on what that method should be. It might be worth noting that when critics write on the subject, such as Harold Bloom in *The Art of Reading Poetry*, there seems to be an emphasis on consciousness of meaning. But when poets try to help us with method—for example Edward Hirsch's *How to Read a Poem and Fall in Love with Poetry*—they lean more toward helping the reader encounter the poem as an experience of intimacy. Part intellectual activity and part emotional response, reading poetry as prayer is going to require both the head and the heart. The reader must actively engage the poet, to collaborate with the poet in making meaning. Poetry is, after all, both written word and spoken word; it is communication using both the mind and the senses. But also the reader's response to the poem goes into and through the emotions, all the way to an intimate relationship with the poet. Hirsch writes,

> I understand the relationship between the poet, the poem, and the reader not as a static entity but as a dynamic unfolding. An emerging sacramental event. A relation between an I and a You. A relational process.

He could as well be describing prayer with God.

If we integrate Bloom's focus on the "consciousness of meaning" and Hirsch's appeal to experience the poem as a "sacramental event," we learn that reading poetry as prayer has much in common with the tradition of *Lectio Divina*, or sacred reading. Prayerful reading of a poem begins with a literal understanding of the text of the poem (or, *lectio*), then moves to an interpretative understanding of the poem – the way its images, symbols, form, and meter all work together to create a "consciousness of meaning" (or, *meditatio*). Although, if we stop here we have merely read a poem. For the poem to become prayer, the reader must respond to the poem's voice, more precisely the source of the poem's voice. In *Lectio Divina*, this stage is called *oratio*. It is also what Hirsch explains as the beginning of the "sacramental event." The final stage in *Lectio Divina*, known as *contemplatio*, describes that state of being the reader reaches when the experience of the poem offers an entry into the ineffable – a state of silent contemplation in the presence of God.

Of course, reading poetry should be a pleasurable experience, and we should be invited into a habit of prayer. Neither should be difficult. A former poet laureate, Billy Collins, warns us we should not "tie the poem up to a chair and torture a confession out of it." Moreover, the saints teach us that prayer comes naturally, if we let it. So, we do not want to make reading poetry as prayer a discipline requiring advanced study and years of spiritual formation. We can all do it, and here are a few practical suggestions for starting.

First, it is important to find good poems. While aesthetic tastes can, and do, vary widely in poetry, the poet's mastery of craft matters. Besides craft, what makes for a good poem? Emily Dickinson, in one of her letters, shared her criteria. "If I read a book and it makes my whole body so cold no fire can warm me, I know that is poetry. If I feel physically as if the top of my head were taken off, I know that is poetry. These are the only ways I know it."

Also, appreciate the poem as a poem. Text becomes poetry when it integrates meaning and imagery experienced through the senses. Begin by reading the poem silently as a way of letting the poem introduce itself – its literal meaning, form, tone, and use of imagery. As Billy Collins says, "hold it up to the light like a color slide . . . ." Next, read the poem out loud to gain an appreciation for the way the poem sounds and how its sound works with its meaning. As Collins says it, "press an ear against its hive." Read again, reflecting upon how the poem communicates through symbols. Once again, Collins has us "drop a mouse into a poem and watch him probe his way out, / or walk inside the poem's room and feel the walls for a light switch."

Next, read the poem as a prayer. Mediate on the images and the symbols. Visualize. Ask yourself how the images and symbols connect with your experience of the holy. Center on a word or phrase and repeat it several times, letting go of your mental response to the poem. Listen to the voice behind the poem.

You can also try to pray like a poet. Poets find their inspiration in the most ordinary of surroundings. Notice the presence of mystery. Think and speak of the holy in metaphors.

Poetry began as an oral tradition, with poems shared in the company of family and friends. A poem shared is an experience of shared intimacy, like praying with someone. Whether read aloud to a soul friend (what the Irish call *anam cara*), or forwarded via e-mail or Facebook post, or given as a gift on a special occasion, a poem can become the medium of communal prayer.

Finally, try to write your own poems of prayer. Choose one of your favorite poems from this anthology. Notice what it is about this poem calling you to the same state of prayer as the poet. Let the poet teach you how.

We compiled this collection of poems not as a textbook on poetry; rather, we intend it to serve as a resource for anyone desiring to approach poetry as a form of prayer. In particular, we have planned it for use in religious retreats by small groups sharing both a faith in God and an appreciation for poetry. Since the anthology is a resource, we arranged the poems thematically to assist the retreat minister in planning a retreat. Still, these poems are more expansive than any of the four categories we used to organize the contents. Any of the poems could have been placed in more than one category, and other possibilities for organizing the poems no doubt will occur to the reader.

Also, we have included some suggestions for discussion, creative writing, and further reading. When arranging these activities, we assumed the retreat minister will have both a passion for poetry and a heart for prayer. Therefore, the resources are not a script; but rather, they are suggestions the retreat minister can tailor for a specific group. Finally, we included more poems than a retreat minister will actually use in a retreat, whether for a weekend or a full week.

The contents are deliberately diverse. In choosing these particular poems we intended to offer variety in their aesthetics, as well as their theologies. Poets from both the Anglican and Roman churches are represented, as well as those poets of whom it can be said are "a church of one" (as was once said of Emily Dickinson). However, all are poets who are well known and have been much loved through the centuries. By doing so, we hope to make the case that much of the poetry we have already read and have grown to appreciate is, indeed, the poetry of prayer.

We also included a brief bibliography of more contemporary poetry collections for readers wanting to pray with poets whose work represents both the aesthetics and experiences of today. Hopefully, this variety will provide the retreat minister with the breadth necessary to plan for groups with varying levels of experience with poetry and divergent points of view on aesthetics. And, more hopefully, it will provide retreat participants with a convenient collection of poems to pray with after a retreat.

In one of his letters, Ranier Maria Rilke writes that his poems were "dictations . . . entrusted" to him. As we read and reflect upon these poems we will see that they too are inspired in the same way as authentic prayer is inspired. Some are songs of praise, others are confessional. Some give thanks while others offer petitions. As such, they run the gamut for the reasons we pray. And, when we experience any of these poems at the same source as the poet's inspiration, we join the poet in prayer.

When is poetry prayer? This anthology attempts to answer the question by example. And, by these examples of poets in prayer we hope our readers might gain stronger appreciation for poetry as a medium for prayer. As a result, we hope readers will deepen their experience of prayer through the medium of poetry.

James Green

What Immortal Hand?

Poems on Images of God

The Pulley

George Herbert

When God at first made man,
Having a glass of blessings standing by,
"Let us," said he, "pour on him all we can.
Let the world's riches, which dispersed lie,
  Contract into a span."

So strength first made a way;
Then beauty flowed, then wisdom, honour, pleasure.
When almost all was out, God made a stay,
Perceiving that, alone of all his treasure,
  Rest in the bottom lay.

"For if I should," said he,
"Bestow this jewel also on my creature,
He would adore my gifts instead of me,
And rest in Nature, not the God of Nature;
  So both should losers be.

"Yet let him keep the rest,
But keep them with repining restlessness;
Let him be rich and weary, that at least,
  If goodness lead him not, yet weariness
  May toss him to my breast."

Love

George Herbert

Love bade me welcome: yet my soul drew back,
      Guilty of dust and sin.
But quick-eyed Love, observing me grow slack
      From my first entrance in,
Drew nearer to me, sweetly questioning
      If I lacked anything.

"A guest," I answered, "worthy to be here":
      Love said, "You shall be he."
"I, the unkind, ungrateful? Ah, my dear,
      I cannot look on thee."
Love took my hand, and smiling did reply,
      "Who made the eyes but I?"

"Truth, Lord; but I have marred them; let my shame
      Go where it doth deserve."
"And know you not," says Love, "who bore the blame?"
      "My dear, then I will serve."
"You must sit down," says Love, "and taste my meat."
      So I did sit and eat.

The Divine Image
William Blake

To Mercy, Pity, Peace, and Love
All pray in their distress;
And to these virtues of delight
Return their thankfulness.

For Mercy, Pity, Peace, and Love
Is God, our father dear,
And Mercy, Pity, Peace, and Love
Is Man, his child and care.

For Mercy has a human heart,
Pity a human face,
And Love, the human form divine,
And Peace, the human dress.

Then every man, of every clime,
That prays in his distress,
Prays to the human form divine,
Love, Mercy, Pity, Peace.

And all must love the human form,
In heathen, Turk, or Jew;
Where Mercy, Love, and Pity dwell
There God is dwelling too.

The Tyger

William Blake

Tyger! Tyger! burning bright
In the forests of the night,
What immortal hand or eye
Could frame thy fearful symmetry?

In what distant deeps or skies
Burnt the fire of thine eyes?
On what wings dare he aspire?
What the hand dare seize the fire?

And what shoulder, & what art.
Could twist the sinews of thy heart?
And when thy heart began to beat,
What dread hand? & what dread feet?

What the hammer? what the chain?
In what furnace was thy brain?
What the anvil? what dread grasp
Dare its deadly terrors clasp?

When the stars threw down their spears,
And watered heaven with their tears,
Did he smile his work to see?
Did he who made the Lamb make thee?

Tyger! Tyger! burning bright
In the forests of the night,
What immortal hand or eye
Dare frame thy fearful symmetry?

This World in Not Conclusion

Emily Dickinson

This World is not Conclusion.
A Species stands beyond—
Invisible, as Music—
But positive, as Sound—
It beckons, and it baffles—
Philosophy—don't know—
And through a Riddle, at the last—
Sagacity, must go—
To guess it, puzzles scholars—
To gain it, Men have borne
Contempt of Generations
And Crucifixion, shown—
Faith slips—and laughs, and rallies—
Blushes, if any see—
Plucks at a twig of Evidence—
And asks a Vane, the way—
Much Gesture, from the Pulpit—
Strong Hallelujahs roll—
Narcotics cannot still the Tooth
That nibbles at the soul—

As Kingfishers Catch Fire

Gerard Manley Hopkins

As kingfishers catch fire, dragonflies draw flame;
As tumbled over rim in roundy wells
Stones ring; like each tucked string tells, each hung bell's
Bow swung finds tongue to fling out broad its name;
Each mortal thing does one thing and the same:
Deals out that being indoors each one dwells;
Selves — goes itself; *myself* it speaks and spells,
Crying *What I do is me: for that I came.*

I say more: the just man justices;
Keeps grace: that keeps all his goings graces;
Acts in God's eye what in God's eye he is —
Chríst — for Christ plays in ten thousand places,
Lovely in limbs, and lovely in eyes not his
To the Father through the features of men's faces.

A Prodigal Son

Chistina Rossetti

Does that lamp still burn in my Father's house,
Which he kindled the night I went away?
I turned once beneath the cedar boughs,
And marked it gleam with a golden ray;
Did he think to light me home some day?

Hungry here with the crunching swine,
Hungry harvest have I to reap;
In a dream I count my Father's kine,
I hear the tinkling bells of his sheep,
I watch his lambs that browse and leap.

There is plenty of bread at home,
His servants have bread enough and to spare;
The purple wine-fat froths with foam,
Oil and spices make sweet the air,
While I perish hungry and bare.

Rich and blessed those servants, rather
Than I who see not my Father's face!
I will arise and go to my Father: -
"Fallen from sonship, beggared of grace,
Grant me, Father, a servant's place."

The Hound of Heaven (excerpt)

Francis Thompson

I fled Him, down the nights and down the days;
  I fled Him, down the arches of the years;
I fled Him, down the labyrinthine ways
  Of my own mind; and in the midst of tears
I hid from Him, and under running laughter.
       Up vistaed hopes I sped;
       And shot, precipitated,
Adown Titanic glooms of chasmed fears,
  From those strong Feet that followed, followed after.
       But with unhurrying chase,
       And unperturbed pace,
   Deliberate speed, majestic instancy,
       They beat—and a Voice beat
       More instant than the Feet—
  'All things betray thee, who betrayest Me'. . . .

Second Coming

William Butler Yeats

Turning and turning in the widening gyre
The falcon cannot hear the falconer;
Things fall apart; the centre cannot hold;
Mere anarchy is loosed upon the world,
The blood dimmed tide is loosed, and everywhere
The ceremony of innocence is drowned;
The best lack all conviction, while the worst
Are full of passionate intensity.

Surely some revelation is at hand;
Surely the Second Coming is at hand.
The Second Coming! Hardly are those words out
When a vast image out of Spiritus Mundi
Troubles my sight: somewhere in sands of the desert
A shape with lion body and the head of a man
A gaze blank and pitiless as the sun,
Is moving its slow thighs, while all about it
Reel shadows of the indignant desert birds.
The darkness drops again; but now I know
That twenty centuries of stony sleep
Were vexed to nightmare by a rocking cradle,
And what rough beast, its hour come round at last,
Slouches toward Bethlehem to be born?

An Orchard for a Dome

Poems on God in Nature

To the Evening Star

William Blake

Thou fair-hair'd angel of the evening,
Now, whilst the sun rests on the mountains, light
Thy bright torch of love; thy radiant crown
Put on, and smile upon our evening bed!
Smile on our loves, and while thou drawest the
Blue curtains of the sky, scatter thy silver dew
On every flower that shuts its sweet eyes
In timely sleep. Let thy west wind sleep on
The lake; speak silence with thy glimmering eyes,
And wash the dusk with silver. Soon, full soon,
Dost thou withdraw; then the wolf rages wide,
And then the lion glares through the dun forest:
The fleeces of our flocks are cover'd with
Thy sacred dew: protect them with thine influence!

It is a Beauteous Evening, Calm and Free
William Wordsworth

It is a beauteous evening, calm and free,
The holy time is quiet as a Nun
Breathless with adoration; the broad sun
Is sinking down in its tranquility;
The gentleness of heaven broods o'er the Sea;
Listen! the mighty Being is awake,
And doth with his eternal motion make
A sound like thunder—everlastingly.
Dear child! dear Girl! that walkest with me here,
If thou appear untouched by solemn thought,
Thy nature is not therefore less divine:
Thou liest in Abraham's bosom all the year;
And worshipp'st at the Temple's inner shrine,
God being with thee when we know it not.

Lines Composed a Few Miles Above Tintern Abbey (excerpt)

William Wordsworth

. . . . For I have learned
To look on nature, not as in the hour
Of thoughtless youth; but hearing oftentimes
The still, sad music of humanity,
Nor harsh nor grating, though of ample power
To chasten and subdue. And I have felt
A presence that disturbs me with the joy
Of elevated thoughts; a sense sublime
Of something far more deeply interfused,
Whose dwelling is the light of setting suns,
And the round ocean and the living air,
And the blue sky, and in the mind of man;
A motion and a spirit, that impels
All thinking things, all objects of all thought,
And rolls through all things. Therefore am I still
A lover of the meadows and the woods,
And mountains; and of all that we behold
From this green earth; of all the mighty world
Of eye, and ear, both what they half create,
And what perceive; well pleased to recognise
In nature and the language of the sense,
The anchor of my purest thoughts, the nurse,
The guide, the guardian of my heart, and soul
Of all my moral being . . . .

To Nature

Samuel Taylor Coleridge

It may indeed be fantasy when I
Essay to draw from all created things
Deep, heartfelt, inward joy that closely clings;
And trace in leaves and flowers that round me lie
Lessons of love and earnest piety.
So let it be; and if the wide world rings
In mock of this belief, it brings
Nor fear, nor grief, nor vain perplexity.
So will I build my altar in the fields,
And the blue sky my fretted dome shall be,
And the sweet fragrance that the wild flower yields
Shall be the incense I will yield to Thee,
Thee only God! and thou shalt not despise
Even me, the priest of this poor sacrifice.

God's Grandeur

Gerard Manley Hopkins

The world is charged with the grandeur of God.
   It will flame out, like shining from shook foil;
   It gathers to a greatness, like the ooze of oil
Crushed. Why do men then now not reck his rod?
Generations have trod, have trod, have trod;
   And all is seared with trade; bleared, smeared with toil;
   And wears man's smudge and shares man's smell: the soil
Is bare now, nor can foot feel, being shod.

And for all this, nature is never spent;
   There lives the dearest freshness deep down things;
And though the last lights off the black West went
   Oh, morning, at the brown brink eastward, springs —
Because the Holy Ghost over the bent
   World broods with warm breast and with ah! bright wings.

Pied Beauty

Gerard Manley Hopkins

Glory be to God for dappled things –
  For skies of couple-colour as a brinded cow;
    For rose-moles all in stipple upon trout that swim;
Fresh-firecoal chestnut-falls; finches' wings;
  Landscape plotted and pieced – fold, fallow, and plough;
    And all trades, their gear and tackle and trim.

All things counter, original, spare, strange;
  Whatever is fickle, freckled (who knows how?)
    With swift, slow; sweet, sour; adazzle, dim;
He fathers-forth whose beauty is past change:
             Praise him.

Some Keep the Sabbath by Going to Church

Emily Dickinson

Some keep the Sabbath going to Church –
I keep it, staying at Home –
With a Bobolink for a Chorister –
And an Orchard, for a Dome –

Some keep the Sabbath in Surplice –
I, just wear my Wings –
And instead of tolling the Bell, for Church,
Our little Sexton – sings.

God preaches, a noted Clergyman –
And the sermon is never long,
So instead of getting to Heaven, at last –
I'm going, all along.

When I Heard the Learn'd Astronomer
Walt Whitman

When I heard the learn'd astronomer,
When the proofs, the figures, were ranged in columns before me,
When I was shown the charts and diagrams, to add, divide,
     and measure them,
When I sitting heard the astronomer where he lectured
     with much applause in the lecture-room,
How soon unaccountable I became tired and sick,
Till rising and gliding out I wander'd off by myself,
In the mystical moist night-air, and from time to time,
Look'd up in perfect silence at the stars.

Birches
Robert Frost

When I see birches bend to left and right
Across the lines of straighter darker trees,
I like to think some boy's been swinging them.
But swinging doesn't bend them down to stay.
Ice-storms do that. Often you must have seen them
Loaded with ice a sunny winter morning
After a rain. They click upon themselves
As the breeze rises, and turn many-colored
As the stir cracks and crazes their enamel.
Soon the sun's warmth makes them shed crystal shells
Shattering and avalanching on the snow-crust,
Such heaps of broken glass to sweep away
You'd think the inner dome of heaven had fallen.
They are dragged to the withered bracken by the load,
And they seem not to break; though once they are bowed
So low for long, they never right themselves:
You may see their trunks arching in the woods
Years afterwards, trailing their leaves on the ground
Like girls on hands and knees that throw their hair
Before them over their heads to dry in the sun.
But I was going to say when Truth broke in
With all her matter-of-fact about the ice-storm
(Now am I free to be poetical?)
I should prefer to have some boy bend them
As he went out and in to fetch the cows,
Some boy too far from town to learn baseball,
Whose only play was what he found himself,
Summer or winter, and could play alone.
One by one he subdued his father's trees
By riding them down over and over again
Until he took the stiffness out of them,
And not one but hung limp, not one was left

For him to conquer. He learned all there was
To learn about not launching out too soon
And so not carrying the tree away
Clear to the ground. He always kept his poise
To the top branches, climbing carefully
With the same pains you use to fill a cup
Up to the brim, and even above the brim.
Then he flung outward, feet first, with a swish,
Kicking his way down through the air to the ground.
So was I once myself a swinger of birches.
And so I dream of going back to be.
It's when I'm weary of considerations,
And life is too much like a pathless wood
Where your face burns and tickles with the cobwebs
Broken across it, and one eye is weeping
From a twig's having lashed across it open.
I'd like to get away from earth awhile
And then come back to it and begin over.
May no fate willfully misunderstand me
And half grant what I wish and snatch me away
Not to return. Earth's the right place for love:
I don't know where it's likely to go better.
I'd like to go by climbing a birch tree,
And climb black branches up a snow-white trunk
Toward heaven, till the tree could bear no more,
But dipped its top and set me down again.
That would be good both going and coming back.
One could do worse than be a swinger of birches.

The Soul in Paraphrase

Poems on Prayer

Canticle

Francis of Assisi

Altissimu, omnipotente, bonsignore,
tue sono le laude,
la Gloria alhonore
et omne benedictione.

Most high, all-powerful, gracious lord,
you are the praise,
the glory and the honor
and every blessing.

Ad te solo, altissimo, se konfano
et nullu homo enne dignu
te mentovare.

They belong to you alone, most high,
and no one is worthy
to speak your name.

Laudato sie, misignore, cum tucte le tue creature,
spetialmente messor lo frate sole,
loquale iorno et allumini noi par loi.

Praise to you, my lord, with all your creatures,
especially Brother Sun,
who begins the day and gives light to us through you.

Et ellu ebellu eradiante cum grande splendore:
de te, altissimo, porta significatione.

And he is beautiful, shining with great splendor
for he heralds you, most high.

Laudato si', misignore, per sora luna ele stele:
in celu lai formate clarite et pretiose et belle.

Praise to you, my Lord, through Sister Moon and Stars.
You have formed them in heaven, pure and precious and beautiful.

Laudato si', misignore, per frate vento,
et per aere et nubilo
et sereno et omne tempo
per loquale a le tue creature
dai sustentamento.

Praise to you, my Lord, through Brother Wind,
through air and cloud,
and calm and all weather
through which you sustain your creation.

Laudato si', misignore, per sor aqua
laquale e multo utile et humile
et pretiosa et cata.

Praise to you, my Lord, through Sister Water,
so very useful and humble
and precious and chaste.

Laudato si', misignore, per frate focu,
per loquale ennalumini la nocte
edello ebello et jocundo
et robustoso et forte.

Praise to you, my Lord, through Brother Fire,
through whom you give light for the night.
And he is handsome and happy,
robust and strong.

Laudato si', misignore, per sora nostra matre terra,
laquale ne sustenta et governa
et produce diversi fructi
con coloriti flori et herba.

Praise to you, my Lord, through our Sister, Mother Earth.
In her sovereignty she sustains us,
Bringing forth all kinds of fruits
And vibrant flowers and herbs.

Translated by James Green

Holy Sonnets No. 14

John Donne

Batter my heart, three-person'd God, for you
As yet but knock, breathe, shine, and seek to mend;
That I may rise and stand, o'erthrow me, and bend
Your force to break, blow, burn, and make me new.
I, like an usurp'd town to another due,
Labor to admit you, but oh, to no end;
Reason, your viceroy in me, me should defend,
But is captiv'd, and proves weak or untrue.
Yet dearly I love you, and would be lov'd fain,
But am betroth'd unto your enemy;
Divorce me, untie or break that knot again,
Take me to you, imprison me, for I,
Except you enthrall me, never shall be free,
Nor ever chaste, except you ravish me.

Denial

George Herbert

When my devotions could not pierce
                    Thy silent ears,
Then was my heart broken, as was my verse;
          My breast was full of fears
                    And disorder.

My bent thoughts, like a brittle bow,
                    Did fly asunder:
Each took his way; some would to pleasures go,
          Some to the wars and thunder
                    Of alarms.

"As good go anywhere," they say,
                    "As to benumb
Both knees and heart, in crying night and day,
          Come, come, my God, O come!
                    But no hearing."

O that thou shouldst give dust a tongue
                    To cry to thee,
And then not hear it crying! All day long
          My heart was in my knee,
                    But no hearing.

Therefore my soul lay out of sight,
                    Untuned, unstrung:
My feeble spirit, unable to look right,
          Like a nipped blossom, hung
                    Discontented.

O cheer and tune my heartless breast,
                    Defer no time;
That so thy favors granting my request,
          They and my mind may chime,
                    And mend my rhyme.

Prayer
George Herbert

Prayer the church's banquet, angel's age,
    God's breath in man returning to his birth,
    The soul in paraphrase, heart in pilgrimage,
The Christian plummet sounding heav'n and earth
Engine against th' Almighty, sinner's tow'r,
    Reversed thunder, Christ-side-piercing spear,
    The six-days world transposing in an hour,
A kind of tune, which all things hear and fear;
Softness, and peace, and joy, and love, and bliss,
    Exalted manna, gladness of the best,
    Heaven in ordinary, man well drest,
The milky way, the bird of Paradise,
    Church-bells beyond the stars heard, the soul's blood,
    The land of spices; something understood.

Savior! I've No One Else to Tell

Emily Dickinson

Savior! I've no one else to tell
And so I trouble thee
I am the one forgot thee so
Dost thou remember me?
Nor, for myself, I came so far
That were the little load
I brought thee the imperial Heart
I had not strength to hold
The Heart I carried in my own
Till mine too heavy grew
Yet—strangest—heavier since it went
Is it too large for you?

Prayer is the Little Implement

Emily Dickinson

Prayer is the little implement
Through which Men reach
Where Presence—is denied them.
They fling their Speech

By means of it—in God's Ear—
If then He hear—
This sums the Apparatus
Comprised in Prayer—

The Pillar of the Cloud

John Henry Newman

Lead, Kindly Light, amid the encircling gloom,
  Lead Thou me on!
The night is dark, and I am far from home—
  Lead Thou me on!
Keep Thou my feet: I do not ask to see
The distant scene—one step enough for me.

I was not ever thus, or pray'd that Thou
  Shouldst lead me on.
I loved to choose and see my path; but now
  Lead Thou me on!
I loved the garish day, and, spite of fears,
Pride ruled my will: remember not past years.

So long Thy power hath blest me, sure it still
  Will lead me on,
O'er moor and fen, o'er crag and torrent, till
  The night is gone;
And with the morn those angel faces smile
Which I have loved long since, and lost awhile.

Evening

John Henry Newman

O Holiest Truth! how have I lied to Thee!
I vow'd this day Thy festival should be:
    But I am dim ere night.
Surely I made my prayer, and I did deem
That I could keep in me Thy morning beam,
    Immaculate and bright.
But my foot slipp'd; and, as I lay, he came,
My gloomy foe, and robbed me of heaven's flame.
Help Thou my darkness, Lord, till I am light.

The Windhover: To Christ Our Lord
Gerard Manley Hopkins

I caught this morning morning's minion, king-
  dom of daylight's dauphin, dapple-dawn-drawn Falcon, in his riding
  Of the rolling level underneath him steady air, and striding
High there, how he rung upon the rein of a wimpling wing
In his ecstasy! then off, off forth on swing,
  As a skate's heel sweeps smooth on a bow-bend: the hurl and gliding
  Rebuffed the big wind. My heart in hiding
Stirred for a bird,—the achieve of; the mastery of the thing!

Brute beauty and valour and act, oh, air, pride, plume, here
  Buckle! AND the fire that breaks from thee then, a billion
Times told lovelier, more dangerous, O my chevalier!

  No wonder of it: sheer plod makes plough down sillion
Shine, and blue-bleak embers, ah my dear,
  Fall, gall themselves, and gash gold-vermillion.

The Lake Isle of Innisfree
William Butler Yeats

I will arise and go now, and go to Innisfree,
And a small cabin build there, of clay and wattles made;
Nine bean-rows will I have there, a hive for the honey-bee,
And live alone in the bee-loud glade.

And I shall have some peace there, for peace comes dropping slow,
Dropping from the veils of the morning to where the cricket sings;
There midnight's all a glimmer, and noon a purple glow,
And evening full of the linnet's wings.

I will arise and go now, for always night and day
I hear lake water lapping with low sounds by the shore;
While I stand on the roadway, or on the pavements grey,
I hear it in the deep heart's core.

The Soul's Expression
Elizabeth Barrett Browning

With stammering lips and insufficient sound
I strive and struggle to deliver right
That music of my nature, day and night
With dream and thought and feeling interwound
And only answering all the senses round
With octaves of a mystic depth and height
Which step out grandly to the infinite
From the dark edges of the sensual ground.
This song of soul I struggle to outbear
Through portals of the sense, sublime and whole,
And utter all myself into the air:
But if I did it,—as the thunder-roll
Breaks its own cloud, my flesh would perish there,
Before that dread apocalypse of soul.

Holy Fire

Poems on Spiritual Growth

The Divine Comedy (excerpt)
Dante Alighieri

I cannot well repeat how there I entered,
　　So full was I of slumber at the moment
　　In which I had abandoned the true way.
But after I had reached a mountain's foot,
　　At that point where the valley terminated,
　　Which had with consternation pierced my heart,
Upward I looked, and I beheld its shoulders,
　　Vested already with that planet's rays
　　Which leadeth others right by every road.
Then was the fear a little quieted
　　That in my heart's lake had endured throughout
　　That night, which I had passed so piteously.

Translated by Henry Wadsworth Longfellow

Surprised by Joy
William Wordsworth

Surprised by joy—impatient as the Wind
I turned to share the transport—Oh! with whom
But Thee, deep buried in the silent tomb,
That spot which no vicissitude can find?
Love, faithful love, recalled thee to my mind—
But how could I forget thee? Through what power,
Even for the least division of an hour,
Have I been so beguiled as to be blind
To my most grievous loss?—That thought's return
Was the worst pang that sorrow ever bore,
Save one, one only, when I stood forlorn,
Knowing my heart's best treasure was no more;
That neither present time, nor years unborn
Could to my sight that heavenly face restore.

Ode on Intimations on Immortality from Recollections of an Early Childhood (excerpt)

William Wordsworth

What though the radiance which was once so bright
Be now for ever taken from my sight,
   Though nothing can bring back the hour
Of splendour in the grass, of glory in the flower;
      We will grieve not, rather find
      Strength in what remains behind;
      In the primal sympathy
      Which having been must ever be;
      In the soothing thoughts that spring
      Out of human suffering;
      In the faith that looks through death,
In years that bring the philosophic mind . . . .

I Know That He Exists

Emily Dickinson

I know that He exists.
Somewhere – in silence –
He has hid his rare life
From our gross eyes.

'Tis an instant's play –
'Tis a fond Ambush –
Just to make Bliss
Earn her own surprise!

But – should the play
Prove piercing earnest –
Should the glee – glaze –
In Death's – stiff – stare –

Would not the fun
Look too expensive!
Would not the jest –
Have crawled too far!

He Fumbles at Your Soul

Emily Dickinson

He fumbles at your Soul
As Players at the Keys
Before they drop full Music on—
He stuns you by degrees—
Prepares your brittle Nature
For the Ethereal Blow
By fainter Hammers—further heard—
Then nearer—Then so slow
Your Breath has time to straighten—
Your Brain—to bubble Cool—
Deals—One—Imperial Thunderbolt—
That scalps your naked Soul—

When Winds take Forests in the Paws—
The Universe—is still—

Uphill
Christina Rossetti

Does the road wind up-hill all the way?
  Yes, to the very end.
Will the day's journey take the whole long day?
  From morn to night, my friend.

But is there for the night a resting-place?
  A roof for when the slow dark hours begin.
May not the darkness hide it from my face?
  You cannot miss that inn.

Shall I meet other wayfarers at night?
  Those who have gone before.
Then must I knock, or call when just in sight?
  They will not keep you standing at that door.

Shall I find comfort, travel-sore and weak?
  Of labour you shall find the sum.
Will there be beds for me and all who seek?
  Yea, beds for all who come.

Sailing to Byzantium
W. B. Yeats

That is no country for old men. The young
In one another's arms, birds in the trees
—Those dying generations—at their song,
The salmon-falls, the mackerel-crowded seas,
Fish, flesh, or fowl, commend all summer long
Whatever is begotten, born, and dies.
Caught in that sensual music all neglect
Monuments of unageing intellect.
An aged man is but a paltry thing,
A tattered coat upon a stick, unless
Soul clap its hands and sing, and louder sing
For every tatter in its mortal dress,
Nor is there singing school but studying
Monuments of its own magnificence;
And therefore I have sailed the seas and come
To the holy city of Byzantium.
O sages standing in God's holy fire
As in the gold mosaic of a wall,
Come from the holy fire, perne in a gyre,
And be the singing-masters of my soul.
Consume my heart away; sick with desire
And fastened to a dying animal
It knows not what it is; and gather me
Into the artifice of eternity.
Once out of nature I shall never take
My bodily form from any natural thing,
But such a form as Grecian goldsmiths make
Of hammered gold and gold enamelling
To keep a drowsy Emperor awake;
Or set upon a golden bough to sing
To lords and ladies of Byzantium
Of what is past, or passing, or to come.

The Road Not Taken
Robert Frost

Two roads diverged in a yellow wood,
And sorry I could not travel both
And be one traveler, long I stood
And looked down one as far as I could
To where it bent in the undergrowth;

Then took the other, as just as fair,
And having perhaps the better claim,
Because it was grassy and wanted wear;
Though as for that the passing there
Had worn them really about the same,

And both that morning equally lay
In leaves no step had trodden black.
Oh, I kept the first for another day!
Yet knowing how way leads on to way,
I doubted if I should ever come back.

I shall be telling this with a sigh
Somewhere ages and ages hence:
Two roads diverged in a wood, and I—
I took the one less traveled by,
And that has made all the difference.

Resources for Planning a Poetry Retreat

by

Sheryl O'Sullivan

IMAGES OF GOD

Scriptural References

Phil 4:8	attributes of God
Ex 3:7-8; Isa 59:19	a liberator
Ps 91:3-4; Lk 13:34	a sheltering bird
Isa 49:15; Isa 66:13	a mother
Mt 3:16-17	a dove
Mt 9:15; Isa 54:5; Rev 21:9	a spouse

Reflection

The poems in this section can illuminate the nature of God in two distinct ways: as attributes of God and as metaphors for God. Let's look at each of these individually.

Attributes of God. Some of the poems in this section discuss attributes of God, and these can be connected to the Scriptural reference in Philippians 4:8. The Blake poem, "The Divine Image" especially focuses on the attributes of God. Blake lists mercy, pity, peace and love as ways in which God's character is made manifest in humanity. Further, Blake states that these attributes *are* God (second stanza), and when they are observed in humans of any sort they are images of God and must be treated with the respect and reverence due God.

St. Paul makes this same point in his letter to the Philippians though he uses slightly different attributes to describe God. In Phil 4:8, Paul uses the words true, honorable, just, pure, pleasing, commendable, excellent and worthy of praise to describe God's character. The attributes Paul chooses are actually a list of Greek virtues which Paul knew the Philippians, who were Greek, would find familiar. As he endeavors to describe the living God of the Jews to this new group of converts, he uses virtuous concepts that are familiar to this group of Greeks. This list, then, is a compilation of some of the most important attributes of God and to contemplate this list, as Paul asks the Philippians to do, is to contemplate the nature of God. St. Paul also adds a concrete bit of advice in the next verse when he instructs the Philippians to think about these attributes in how they have seen Paul behave if thinking about them in terms of God in general is too abstract to be helpful. In asking the Philippians to think about these attributes, Paul is not just exhorting them to become Pollyanna types who naively keep the good thought regardless of circumstances. He has a deeper purpose for asking his converts in Philippi to think on these attributes. Assuming our goal as humans is to emulate God, we will not be able to do this successfully unless we discover God's nature and think consistently about the attributes of God's character. Gaining dominion over our thoughts and turning them consistently toward congruence with God's thoughts is a first step toward becoming more like God in our daily lives.

Metaphors for God. Many of the poems in this section suggest metaphors for God. Yeats, for example, describes God as having a lion's body and the head of a man, as being a rough beast. Emily Dickinson describes God as a species standing beyond the world, while Thompson thinks of God as a pursuing hound.

The Bible also uses metaphor freely to endeavor to describe this huge and indescribable being known as God. Many of the Scripture references listed above employ metaphor to describe some facet of God. Images as diverse as a powerful liberator and a brood hen are used to explain to us just a bit of what God is like. As C.S. Lewis once suggested in a sermon entitled, "Transpositions," the language of God and the language of humans is so far apart that it is very difficult at times for God to communicate with us. The use of metaphor is one way in which God tries to tell us things about himself that are deeper than our human language can accommodate. God uses nature and concrete images to illuminate spiritual or abstract teachings for our finite minds. For example, God uses various images of birds to reveal different aspects of his character to us. God variously refers to himself as a sheltering bird, a hen and a dove in different parts of the Old and New Testaments (see above). Picturing God as a mother hen who abandons all dignity in order to lovingly collect her wayward brood and bring them to safety close to her body, sheltered by her wings is a very comforting image of God. Seeing God as a dove that symbolizes peace and speaks of his pleasure in his Son is also comforting. Another metaphor often used is that of a spouse. Thinking of God in this way, as a spouse who provides a safe haven, who cares for your well-being, who encourages you to grow, who shares your private jokes and your history, or in any of the other ways in which we think of a spouse goes a long way in bringing the abstractness of a loving and intimate God down to a concreteness we humans can understand.

Attribute lists and metaphors are very useful for discovering the nature of God, and both Scripture and poetry contain many examples of these that can be used in a retreat setting. The poems and Scripture verses listed here are only a beginning. It is important, though, that we not confuse image with essence. God is more than a list of characteristics, and more than a concrete image however inclusive these may attempt to be. God is always more. We use lists and metaphors to examine a small piece of God with our finite minds, but we should not confuse this small piece with the totality of God.

Discussion

The following questions may be useful in moving the discussion of the nature of God forward.

❖ What images of God are the most helpful to me now? Why are they so helpful?

❖ What images of God have I outgrown? Why are these no longer so useful for me?

❖ What people have presented for me a human image of God? How did they help me know God better?

❖ How could I use my own images to expand or improve my awareness of God?

❖ What attributes would I add to Blake's attribute list if I were describing God? To Paul's list?

❖ What attributes of God do I need to think upon more diligently and try to follow more closely?

Suggested Activities

❖ Often terms mean different things to different people. In Phil 4:8 the list of attributes describing God is not always translated in the same way. A word study is a particularly helpful activity to do with this list. Simply list the attributes as given in your own translation of the Bible. Then ask participants to look in their own Bibles, which are often other translations, for the words that take the place of the ones in your Bible. For example, the word "honorable" used in one translation is rendered as "worthy," "venerable," and "noble" in other translations. These different terms often offer slightly different connotations which are useful for discussion. If one term is generally translated in the same way in all versions, you can go to the dictionary for additional ideas. It works well to do this exercise in writing either on a chalkboard or on chart paper.

❖ A quick-write is often a good way to get participants thinking before asking them to join discussions or small group activities. Writing for 5-10 minutes on a prompt such as, "How would you describe God?" before beginning work with the poems allows participants to tap into their own thoughts before entertaining the thoughts of others.

❖ When dealing with the images of God, it is especially helpful to incorporate artwork which gives visual images of God. This may be artwork that has gained recognition, such as Michelangelo's Pieta, or it can be artwork that participants themselves create in response to the images of God offered in the poetry you discuss.

Ritual

Close the retreat with a ritual that brings the subject of the retreat close to the participants in a way that is different from the intellectual examinations they have had of the subject during the rest of the day. Here is a suggested ritual that asks participants to continue to consider the nature of God.

❖ Light a prayer candle and put on very soft music— something on the order of a Gregorian chant.

❖ Give the following prompts slowly allowing participants to gradually enter a deeper space:

- *Close your eyes and breathe deeply for a few seconds.*
- *Bring to mind a person who represents an image of God for you.*
- *What about this person is Godlike? Visualize this.*

- *What can you know about God from having this person in your mind?*
- *Quietly contemplate this person.*
- *Rest in this person's presence.*
- *Be happy and peaceful with this person.*
- *Now let the Godlike part of this person lead you toward God.*
- *See God as clearly as you saw that human person.*
- *See God's image. What is God like?*
- *Rest in God's presence.*
- *Be happy and peaceful here.*
- *Adore God.*
- *Adore God.*
- *Now ask God how you might be more like God.*
- *Listen to God. Attend to God.*
- *Thank God for his almighty presence.*
- *Now slowly come back to this room.*
- *Bring God's peace and attention with you.*
- *Breathe deeply.*
- *Open your eyes.*
- *Smile gently at the image of God sitting next to you.*

Closing Prayer

Merciful and beautiful God, we adore you with all our hearts. We thank you for your loving presence to us, and we thank you for the beautiful images of yourself that you have made clear to us today. Help us to take these images of you out into our daily and confusing world. Help us to live as you would live and act as you would act in all of our dealings with other people at least for this day. Help us to see your image in others, especially our enemies where we find it so hard to see, and especially in our families where we see it but fail to respect it as we want to. Finally, we ask you to please conform us to yourself to such an extent that others will see you clearly in us. We ask all of this in Jesus' name. Amen

Extension Activities

❖ Participants may want to continue the activities that were begun during the retreat. For example, those who have started a piece of visual art will want to complete it, and those who have begun writing about the nature of God may want to continue this writing.

❖ During the meditation, participants may feel that God has come to them in a special way, and they way want to write down the ways in which they thought that God especially wanted them to be more like him. Contemplation of these could be ongoing.

❖ Now that participants have looked at the images of God in several poems and several Bible verses, they may want to try to compose some poetry of their own based upon their individual images of God as exposed during the discussions of the retreat.

❖ For further reading, participants may be interested in reading C.S. Lewis' complete sermon, "Transpositions." They may also be interested in reading *Your God is Two Small* by Phillip Yancey, which deals with metaphors of God that we have outgrown.

GOD IN NATURE

Scriptural References

Mountains:	Ex 19:3-25	1 Kings 19:11-15
	Ps 121:1-2	Isa 52:7
	Mt 4:8	Mk 9:2-8
Wilderness:	1 Kings 19:4-7	Isa 51:3
	Mk 1:4, 35	Mk 6:31-32
	Lk 4:1-2	Mt 4:1-2
Water:	Gen 8:1-5	Jonah 2:3
	Ps 36:6	Ps 69:1-2
	Ps 77:19	Ps 104:25-26
General:	Gen 3:8 (garden)	Mt 26:39 (garden)
	Mt 6:28-30 (fields)	
	Ps 65:12-13 (valleys and meadows)	
	Isa 40:3 (many settings)	

Reflection

The poems in this section all highlight the importance of natural settings in bringing us closer to God. Some of the poets used very specific images to refer to God's presence, such as Hopkins' tribute to speckled things in nature, or Whitman's use of the stars to call forth God after listening too long to man. Other poets like Blake, Dickinson and Coleridge, recognized that nature can serve as well as a church as a place of worship. Still other selections speak to the overall majesty of God as when Hopkins exclaimed, "The world is charged with the grandeur of God." Finally, Wordsworth perhaps defined God's use of nature best when he remarked that a lovely evening shows, "God being with thee when we know it not."

As Emerson said, "Natural facts are symbols of spiritual facts." Mankind has used the physical world of nature as a portal to God since the time of Genesis when God walked in the garden in the cool of the evening (Gen 3:8). Many aspects of nature are mentioned in Scripture. Examples of some of these references are given above and include verses referring to the desert/wilderness, seas/oceans, fields, gardens, valleys, meadows, hills and mountains. In this reflection, we will focus on the references to mountains, but you could easily focus on any of the other areas of nature if this is more appropriate for your group.

Three of the Scripture verses given above that refer to mountains tell about times when God met man on one of the mountains. In Exodus 19:3-25 we see Moses meeting God on Mt. Sinai to receive the 10 Commandments. In 1Kings 19:11-15 we see Elijah going up onto Mt. Horeb to meet God. And in Mark 9:2-8 we have the Transfiguration in which Jesus communes with God the Creator and the prophets before the astonished eyes of the disciples. Clearly, if we would like to meet God, the mountain is the place to go! But what is it about the mountain that might place us in the presence of God?
Literally the mountain is no closer to God than other locations. We all know it is not possible to build a "stairway to heaven" and climbing to a higher altitude puts you no closer in space to God. So if it isn't literal closeness in space that a mountain can offer, what could it offer us metaphorically about drawing nearer to God?

Anyone who has ever hiked in the mountains knows that the metaphors come quickly during the ascent as if the thinner air makes it easier to breathe in the essence of God. For example, mountain climbing is never easy. Even when it begins with ease, it will soon enough be demanding all our strength to carry on. Often we lose sight of the trail and become disoriented. Sometimes we must go down to go up, and go back to go onward. This is not the way we want it to be. We want life to be easy, straight forward and understandable. We want God to be this way, too. Yet, what we are really asking is that God conform to our finite abilities. Just as the mountain will not remake itself for our ease, so God will not limit himself to make our journey to him more effortless. Sometimes we will be disoriented; sometimes we will have to go back to go on. To ask that God flatten himself for our convenience is to ask God to cease to be God. We don't really want that.

Yet, God, immeasurably more immense than any mountain we can imagine, wants to meet us. God invites us to the high places, just as Moses and Elijah and Jesus were also invited. And something within us wants to go there, though we know it will be a difficult climb. We do not want to be like the ancient Israelites who were so awed by the sight of God that they withdrew and begged Moses to be their intermediary (Ex 20:18-21). We want the transformation that a meeting with God promises. We know that it is the challenge of the climb up the mountain that gives our lives vigor. We grow toward that transformative meeting with God with every steep path, every rocky patch, every deep chasm we face and conquer. Ease is not the promise of God; transformation is the promise of God. Mountains can be a metaphor, a way of coming to a deeper understanding, of what this journey toward God entails. Challenging, yes, but infinitely rewarding.

Discussion

The following questions may be useful in moving the discussion of nature and God forward.

❖ Where do you most regularly see God in nature? The ocean? The mountains? A cornfield? A meadow?

❖ What is the metaphor of God that this place brings to your mind?

❖ Besides the image of climbing in mountains, what other lessons from God could mountains bring forth for you?

❖ Call to mind a time when nature burst upon you and you exclaimed as Hopkins did, "The world is charged with the grandeur of God." What was the scene that produced this in you? How were you changed by this event?

❖ Now call to mind a time when God's presence was made known to you in a much less awesome way, such as Coleridge describes in the "trace of leaves and flowers". What did you learn about God in these more quiet displays of nature?

❖ How can you use these various metaphors and visions of God in nature to expand your own growing awareness of God's being?

Suggested Activities

❖ A retreat using the theme of God in Nature should not all be spent inside. If it is at all possible, the group should go outside for a time of quiet meditation in whatever nature is available at the site. Instruct participants to go alone to whatever place draws them and spend some silent time meditating on God as they look at nature. Journaling could also be done at this time.

❖ Using the inspiration participants have gotten from being out in nature, ask everyone to write a poem of their own. A good way to introduce this activity is to look at the form of the following poem of Emily Dickinson.

> I never saw a moor,
> I never saw the sea;
> Yet, know I how the heather looks,

And what a wave must be.

I never spoke with God,
Nor visited in heaven;
Yet certain am I of the spot
As if the chart were given.

This poem is written using quatrains that upon closer analysis are rhyming couplets with line breaks in the middle—the first lines are twelve syllables and the second lines are fourteen syllables. Emily Dickinson used this form, or some variation of it, in nearly all her poems. Have participants practice writing couplets that focus on a particular image. They may then move to combining these, as Dickinson has, into actual poems about using nature to understand God.

❖ The haiku lends itself to meditations on nature. This ancient Japanese form of poetry has three lines. The first line has five syllables, the second line has seven syllables, and the third line has five syllables again. This type of poem seeks to find the essential quality or deep essence of something in nature. Often Haiku poems are seasonal and offer an insight into some aspect of nature. Have participants practice writing haiku poems that focus on particular images in nature that they feel reveals God's presence. These can also be illustrated if desired. A good source book for writing haiku is the book, *If Not for the Cat* by Jack Prelutsky.

Ritual

Close the retreat with a ritual that brings the subject of the retreat close to the participants in a way that is different from the intellectual examinations they have had of the subject during the rest of the day. Here is a suggested ritual that asks participants to continue to consider how nature is but a finite symbol of the greatness of God.

Give each participant a small stone or pebble. Tell them this is to represent our most terrible and oppressive worries-the ones we brought into the retreat today, and pray about with the most fervor. Now take participants out to whatever nature is available to you at your site. Try to make this as grand a vista of nature as you can find, but even small bits of nature can be used if necessary. Tell participants to look on the wonders of nature before them and to meditate on the vastness of God's being which is far greater than even this vast natural setting. Remind participants that God's being is infinite, but also God's care is infinite. Ask them to take their pebble and give it into God's hands by leaving it outside in the natural setting. This should be done slowly, with faithfulness, reminding ourselves as we lay our burdens down that God's infinite care can take these burdens from us.

Closing Prayer

Great and wondrous God, we bring our cares, our needs, our very lives to you. We thank you for your tremendous glory and for giving us nature to help us understand that glory. Help us increase our faith that we may know your power and your love more completely. Help us to truly believe that you can take our many burdens from us, and that we can rest in you. Give us the peace that comes from this true faith in you. As we prepare to go back to our daily lives, help us to remember to look at nature and think of you and know your peace. Amen

Extension Activities

❖ Participants may want to continue the poetry activity that they began during the retreat. Most people will probably need more time to complete the Dickinson-type poem satisfactorily, and some participants may wish to continuing working on this.

❖ The only scripture verses to be addressed in this retreat reflection are those having to do with mountains. The other areas of nature mentioned in scripture are equally valuable to seeing God. Participants may want to choose a different venue of nature (sea, garden, etc.) and examine the verses given that refer to that area. They then may want to write a reflection of their own using some or all of these verses. The reflection using the verses about mountains could be used as a model.

❖ During their quiet time out in nature, participants may feel that some of the thoughts they had or journal entries they made deserve further reflection. Contemplation of these could be ongoing.

❖ For further reading, participants may be interested in reading Ralph Waldo Emerson's essay, *Nature*. They might also enjoy Hannah Hurnard's *Hind's Feet on High Places*.

PRAYER

Scriptural References

The Efficacy of Prayer:	Mt 7:7	Mk 11:24
	Lk 11:9-13	Jn 16:24
Attitudes in Prayer:	Lk 11:5-8 (perseverance)	
	1 Thess 5:17 (constancy)	
	Lk 18:1-8 (perseverance)	
	Lk 18:9-14 (humility)	
	Rom 12:12 (perseverance)	
How to Pray:	Mt 6:6 (privacy)	
	Mk 1:35 (privacy)	
	Lk 11:2-4 (Our Father)	

Reflection

In Scripture the subject of prayer comes up over and over again. We can sense in the apostles the same feelings we have ourselves about how to best pray, and we also see their attention to the question of whether and how prayer is valuable. These questions and concerns seem to be universal and timeless. We still question, just as the apostles did, whether prayer works and if so is there a "best" way to do it. Just as in Jesus' time, questions about prayer occupy our minds. They also have occupied the minds of the poets in this section. While the poems differ significantly in style and content, each poet is trying diligently to discover and communicate some important truth about prayer.

The poems in this section can be roughly divided into the three areas listed above in the Scriptural references. First and foremost, we question, as does Herbert, whether prayer works. This must have been a very big question in Jesus' time, too because all four of the gospel writers take pains to assure us that indeed prayer does work. The four gospels have a relatively rare point of near congruence when all four evangelists say essentially, "Ask and you shall receive." Each puts a slightly different wording on the concept, with different parables and examples used to illustrate the point. And John adds that we should not only ask, but ask in the name of Jesus. But essentially, the message that prayer is valuable and brings results is repeated with confidence in all four gospels. We do not gain insights from the evangelists as to exactly how prayer works. And the poems in this section make note that sometimes prayer works in ways we do not understand, and in ways we find it hard to articulate. Poets, apostles, theologians and we have consistently tried to pin down exactly how prayers are answered with varying degrees of success. Still Scripture is not vague about the efficacy of prayer. Prayers are answered. We need only ask to be certain of that.

The second attribute of prayer that is consistently addressed in both Scripture and poetry is the correct attitudes that should be present for prayer that is pleasing to God. Several scriptural verses stress that perseverance and constancy are necessary for righteous prayer, with Paul writing to the Thessalonians to "pray without ceasing". This ceaseless prayer is especially important in times of adversity when it appears that God is absent, inattentive or uncaring. Herbert's poem, "Denial" addresses the emotions of apparently unheeded prayer when he writes, "When my devotions could not pierce Thy silent ears; then was my heart broken, as was my verse." We have all had the "dry bones" times when prayer seems empty, or worse, the "dark night of the soul" periods when prayer seems absurd. The necessity of continuing in faith despite the outward appearance that prayer is not bringing results is the reason perseverance in prayer is mentioned so regularly by the apostles. Beyond constancy, though, there is also the matter of appropriate posture before God as we approach him in prayer. Luke reminds us that humility is the foremost attitude we should have when approaching God. The well-known story contrasting the Pharisee who prayed thanking God he was not like other people with the tax collector who begged for God's forgiveness in Luke 18:9-14 is a clear indication of the attitude of humility that God wants from us in prayer. Donne states this humble posture poetically when he entreats God to "o'erthrow me, and bend your force to break, blow, burn, and make me new."

Finally, the apostles pressed Jesus, just as we do, for a basic how-to manual on the best methods for prayer. Jesus obliged his apostles both in word and in action. In action, he made prayer a focus of his life, and we are told he periodically went off by himself to a lonely place to pray. The importance of solitude in prayer is underscored in the gospels of both Matthew and Mark. Jesus' clearest words about prayer, though, are reported in Luke 11:2-4. In this passage, Jesus teaches his disciples the words to what we now call The Lord's Prayer or The Our Father. As Jesus' clearest teaching on how to pray, this prayer bears careful study.

One well-known formula for praying uses the acronym, ACTS, to help us remember the various parts of prayer. The letters in ACTS stand for "adoration, confession, thanksgiving and supplication." As we analyze the words of "Our Father" (also, "The Lord's Prayer") we find that it does, indeed, include all four parts of ACTS. Jesus starts with adoration when he says that God's name is hallowed. St. Francis' poem of praise also stresses this adoration. The Our Father gives attention to confession in the words, "forgive us our trespasses." Newman's "The Pillar of the Cloud" echoes this in the words, "I was not ever thus, nor pray'd that Thou shouldst lead me on. I loved to choose and see my path, but now lead Thou me on!" Thanksgiving is found in the "Lord's Prayer" in the words, "thy kingdom come" and Yeats speaks thankfully of the peace that comes "dropping slow" in his poem, "The Lake Isle of Innisfree."

Finally, The Our Father is filled with supplication when Jesus teaches us to present our needs to the Father by saying, "give us this day our daily bread" and "deliver us from evil." Dickinson's poem goes to the core of supplication when she says she brought her heart to God because it became too heavy for her to carry on her own.

Simone Weil said, "The 'Our Father' contains all possible petitions; we cannot conceive of any prayer not already contained in it. It is to prayer what Christ is to humanity." As we consider the topic of prayer through poetry we might do well to begin with this perfect prayer that Jesus left us. We will also want to explore, though, the other insights about prayer that are available to us in Scripture and articulated for us in many profound ways in the poetry in this section.

Discussion

The following questions may be useful in moving the discussion of spiritual growth forward.

❖ Using the references above in all four gospels that point to the efficacy of prayer, compare the wording of the four versions. What additional insights might be gained from the different ways in which the evangelists phrased the common thought that prayer is answered?

❖ Several of the poems speak of despair and the difficulty of prayer during these times. In what circumstances have you found prayer to be especially difficult? How were you able to persevere in prayer? In retrospect, were there things you learned during this time?

❖ Yeats' speaks of the need for peace "in the deep heart's core." What ways have you found that are useful in taking you to a place of peace so that your prayer can be fruitful? Do you have a particular prayer space or ritual that could be helpful to others?

❖ Newman's poem, "Evening" deals with the universal problem of not being true to our own prayers. Newman says he started the day with bright promise and good intentions, but ended the day "robb'd of heaven's flame". Why do you think we find it so hard to keep our good intensions? Can prayer be helpful here or would we be better off not making such grand promises?

❖ Discuss the statement in Czeslaw Milosz's poem "Readings", "thus on every page a persistent reader sees twenty centuries as twenty days." What does this mean to you? How could you use this statement to enhance your own prayer life?

Suggested Activities

❖ Using the ACTS formula given in the meditation for this section, choose one of the four areas to examine in depth. Choose poems, in this book or elsewhere, that have to do with either adoration, confession, thanksgiving or supplication. Look at the different ways the poets address the theme. What styles, words or phrases resonate with participants as they examine one area of prayer in more depth? Ask participants to compose a poem of their own about this same theme using the retreat poems as models or inspiration.

❖ Much of our prayer is personal, silent prayer, but we also have oral, communal prayer at various times. The poems in this section can be used to combine the aspects of communal prayer and oral interpretation. Have participants meet in groups to choose one poem or portion of a poem to read aloud to the group. Different people will naturally give different oral interpretations to the passage as they read it aloud. These differences should then be discussed in the groups to discover what new meanings were made available by the different interpretations.

❖ Midrash is an ancient Jewish technique of Bible study in which a phrase or portion of a story is expanded upon by the interpreter in order to gain greater insights into the meaning of this passage. Take one of the scriptural passages listed above and ask participants to journal briefly on what this passage might mean to them. Then write a short story or poem relating to that passage that expands its meaning.

❖ Using the ACTS formula discussed earlier, have participants compose a brief prayer of their own. These prayers may be shared orally at the end of the day or could be placed together in a booklet available to all participants.

❖ There are numerous methods of prayer that can be discussed and used throughout the retreat time. Besides the ACTS formula, another method of prayer is to have participants sit quietly with an open Bible and read whatever they like. They should read along until something causes their mind to stop and contemplate. Whatever this part is, participants should write it down on the top of a piece of paper then sit quietly and converse with God about this phrase. What is it that God would like to say about this passage? Participants may want to practice this method at some point during the retreat day, and then journal about what it was that God revealed to them as they sat quietly and listened.

❖ Solitude and silence are stressed in several scripture passages and poems pertaining to prayer. Solitude and silence are hard to practice in a large retreat, and even harder to practice during daily life. Give participants some time during this retreat to seek a place a relative solitude and pray in silence on their own. A retreat about prayer that does not include an opportunity for solitary prayer seems to be missing the point in some way.

Ritual

Close the retreat with a ritual that brings the subject of the retreat close to the participants in a way that is different from the intellectual examinations they have had of the subject during the rest of the day.

Here is a suggested ritual that asks participants to practice a type of prayer that is known as centering prayer. During this prayer time participants should sit comfortably and quietly wherever they wish. They should quiet their minds and bodies by breathing deeply several times and closing their eyes. They should then wait in a receptive way for God to direct them. To do this they should clear their minds of all extraneous thought, and contemplate God. Since our minds are prone to wander, however, each participant should choose a prayer word to repeat in order to bring his or her mind back to contemplation of God. Examples of prayer words could be, *Jesus*, *love* or *Abba*. Participants should gently repeat this word whenever they notice their minds have wandered. For this ritual, allow participants to stay in this meditative state for at least 10 minutes. This will seem like a long time to people who are not used to this sort of prayer. However, as participants grow accustomed to centering prayer, they should be instructed to try to stay in this type of prayer for about 20-30 minutes twice per day. After about 10 minutes of silence today, gently call participants' attention back to the group. They should keep their eyes closed for another minute or two as they allow their minds to gently rejoin the group. While this is happening, the leader can close with the following prayer.

Let us pray:

Dear God, we love you with all our hearts. You are the center of our lives, the center of our every desire. We worship your holy name. We close now by praying together the perfect prayer that Jesus gave us:

Our Father, who art in heaven, hallowed be thy name. Thy kingdom come; thy will be done, on earth as it is in Heaven. Give us this day our daily bread. And forgive us our trespasses as we forgive those who trespass against us. And lead us not into temptation, but deliver us from evil. Amen

Extension Activities

❖ Participants may want to continue the poetry or prayer writing activities that they began during the retreat. Most people will probably need more time to complete these creative works satisfactorily, and some participants may wish to continuing working on this.

❖ Only a few of the scriptural verses listed are addressed in the reflection and the activities for this retreat. Participants may want to choose a different set of scriptural verses to examine. They then may want to write a reflection of their own using some or all of these verses.

❖ Participants may want to learn more about centering prayer and begin to practice it or other forms of contemplative prayer in their daily lives. They can learn more about centering prayer by consulting the following books:

- Fr. Thomas Keating, *Open Mind, Open Heart*
- Fr. Basil Pennington, *An Invitation to Centering Prayer*

❖ For further reading, participants may also be interested in reading the following books on the topic of prayer:

- Fr. Thomas H. Green, *Prayer and Common Sense*
- St. John of the Cross, *Dark Night of the Soul*
- Brother Laurence and Frank Laubach, *Practicing His Presence*
- C. S. Lewis, *Letters to Malcolm: Chiefly on Prayer*
- Thomas Merton, *Thoughts in Solitude*
- Henri J.M. Nouwen, *Life of the Beloved*
- Karl Rahner, *Encounters with Silence*

SPIRITUAL GROWTH AND DEVELOPMENT

Scriptural References

General Spiritual Growth:	Col 1:9-10	2 Pet 3:18
	Col 2:18-19	Sir 1:1
	Prov 13:20	Ecc 2:13-14
Spiritual Gifts:	Rom 12:6-8	1 Cor 12:4-11
	1 Cor 12:28	Eph 4:11
Growth and Suffering	2 Cor 6:9-10	1 Pet 1:6-7
	Col 1:24	Wis 3:1-7
	Ecc 1:18	Book of Job

Reflection

Each of the poems in this section deals with spiritual growth and development in some way, yet they are quite different from one another and follow three distinct themes. Several of the poems discuss general spiritual growth especially looking at rites of passage and developmental stages. Dickinson's "He Fumbles at Your Soul" and Yeats' "Sailing to Byzantium" both look at various stages of life and the growth associated with these stages. A second theme in the poems is the value of finding our own ways in our spiritual quests. Frost's "Road Not Taken" and Dickinson's "I Know that He Exists" both consider this theme. Finally, many of the poems in this section consider suffering and its role in spiritual growth. Donne, Rossetti and Wordsworth all explore sorrow as a means of moving toward God. Judging from the themes of these poems we might conclude that while spiritual growth has elements of commonality, it is essentially an individual endeavor that will inevitably involve pain and suffering. In this reflection we will examine these three themes.

There is a bumper sticker that reads, "What you are is God's gift to you; what you become is your gift to God." While getting any worthwhile message down to bumper-sticker size is sometimes dangerous, there is much wisdom to this sentiment. We can look around and easily see that God has made us different from one another. Sometimes this makes us joyful, but many times this is a cause for strife. Yet, we understand and believe that God did not make us capriciously or in error. God meant for us to each have the very gifts and attributes we possess. Knowing this, we must ask ourselves, "What are the gifts God has given me, and how am I to use them for God's glory?"

Scripture mentions spiritual gifts several times in the New Testament. While these lists of gifts differ somewhat, they are a good way to begin to consider what God has given us and what we might make of it. Romans 12:6-8, for instance, lists such gifts as prophecy, teaching, serving, giving, and compassion as gifts of the Spirit. We might ask where our own particular strengths are in this list and what life experiences have brought these gifts to light and sharpened them.

Sometimes these life experiences are organized around particular rites of passage or rituals. Often, though, these experiences are outside of collective rituals and instead can show us the personal guiding hand of God in our individual lives. Looking at the specific ways in which God has shepherded us personally can be very enlightening in discerning God's plan for us.

It is often helpful, too, to put these experiences into some sort of theoretical framework. J. Robert Clinton, in his book *The Making of a Leader*, offers a simple framework that can be used for this purpose. In Clinton's timeline of leadership development he lists stages that God uses to enhance our spiritual growth. These stages are: "Sovereign Foundations," in which personal character is developed; "Inner-Life Growth," in which training and mentoring take place; "Ministry Maturing," in which early attempts at being useful to God's plan take place; "Life Maturing," in which particular gifts and combinations of gifts are identified and used more fully; and "Convergence" in which a person's gifts, temperament and abilities are all fully used by God. Clinton believes that during the first three stages God is working *in* an individual, and it is not until the last two stages that God is really using an individual and working *through* that person. By placing own journeys on this theoretical timeline we can notice the very intentional ways in which God has made and groomed us for service.

Finding God's hand in our lives can be very helpful to us in our spiritual growth, but beyond this help, it can also be very comforting to look back and see the presence of God in our lives especially during periods of trials and sorrow. In looking at the experiences we would individually chart on Clinton's timeline there will certainly be events, experiences and conditions that we would not choose because they are too painful. Yet, in looking back through these we begin to recognize that suffering is a particular aspect of spiritual growth. All of us have noticed this at one time or another. Poets write about it (many are referenced in this section), and Scripture devotes many verses and one whole book (Job) to the problem of suffering.

We do not want spiritual growth to be painful. We do not want this to be the way it is. We repeatedly in life ask God if he is sure he knows what he is doing. We imply that we could do a better job of it, or at least a less painful one. Job is our role model for this. Job is a good man, yet he cries out to God for an explanation of his trials (Job 30:16-23). We do not want to endure trials, but if they must be endured, we at least want to make sense of them.

This problem of pain, as C.S. Lewis calls it, is in large part a problem of meaning. Philip Yancey notes in his book *Where is God When it Hurts* that humans will endure a great deal of pain when they can see that it has meaning. He gives the example of women who willingly undergo the pain of childbirth because of the meaningful purpose it has. In considering this, especially as it relates to spiritual growth, it can be comforting to look back in life to see where the hand of God has been guiding us especially during our trials. Doing this can also help us to make meaning of these sorrowful times.

If we fail to make meaning and grow spiritually from suffering, pain remains only pain. Knowing this is often of very little consolation to us, though, when we are in the midst of a sorrowful time. Yet the consolation can come later, as we process these events and experiences. Theoretical techniques like Clinton's timeline can be helpful in this, and the metaphorical and cathartic attributes of poetry are perfectly suited to helping us make meaning from our experiences and grow from them. Since pain is wasted if we fail to learn from it, our spiritual development and well-being depend upon us learning as much as we can from every experience, especially the painful ones.

Discussion

The following questions may be useful in moving the discussion of spiritual growth forward.

❖ Using the spiritual gifts listed in Romans 12:6-8 or one of the other scriptural lists, what gifts might God have bestowed upon you in abundance? Do you have other gifts besides those listed?

❖ In what ways have you found your individual path for spiritual development as Frost and Dickinson advised? What sort of sacrifices have you had to make to do this?

❖ What do you think are the benefits of communal rites of passage such as Confirmation or Bar Mitzvah? What have some of your beneficial rites of passage been? How were you changed?

❖ In Christina Rossetti's poem she says the road is uphill all the way to the very end. This is not a very pleasant thought from a human perspective. Why do you think God allows the way to be so steep?

❖ Discuss the statement, "Pain is wasted if you fail to learn from it." What does this mean to you? How could we use this statement for our own spiritual growth?

Suggested Activities

❖ Look at the spiritual gifts listed in one of the scriptural references. Do a double entry journal to help with meditation on these gifts. To do the double entry journal, have participants draw a line down the middle of a sheet of paper. On the left side of the line have people list the gifts they think they have. Then on the right side of the paper have members of the group list how each of these gifts might be used in their lives to further God's plan.

❖ There are four different lists of spiritual gifts listed in the scriptural references for this section. The lists have some overlap but also contain some differences. An interesting exercise for discussing spiritual gifts is to make a chart of the gifts listed in all four references and compare these lists. Since the lists do not agree completely we can also assume that there may be more gifts than those listed. After comparing the four lists, add new gifts that participants have noticed in themselves and others. Why do they believe these are spiritual gifts?

❖ Look at Clinton's timeline once again. Put his 5 stages on a handout. Have participants fill in the specific events in their own lives in the appropriate spaces on the timeline. You may also want to have participants reflect through journaling on some of the events they have listed.

❖ Pain needs to be examined when possible so that it is mined for every possible bit of learning and meaning. This is best done after the most acute time of suffering has passed and people are capable of taking a more "philosophic mind," as Wordsworth wrote in his "Ode on Intimations of Immortality from Recollections of an Early Childhood." A good way to examine pain for meaning is through journaling. Have participants journal about one time of steep growth that was brought about by suffering. First have group members write about the actual event. Then ask them to list 2 or 3 things that they identified as lessons from this time. Finally, ask participants to sit quietly for a while with this memory and consider whether they might be able to identify one more lesson that has come to them as they have considered the event from a more distant perspective.

❖ Ask participants to choose one of the poems listed in this section of the anthology or another of their own choosing. Ask them to relate the insights in this poem to a specific event in their lives. Some participants may want to use this poem as a model for writing a poem of their own about this event.

Ritual

Close the retreat with a ritual that brings the subject of the retreat close to the participants in a way that is different from the intellectual examinations they have had of the subject during the rest of the day. Here is a suggested ritual that asks participants to continue to consider how God is working in and through them through the gifts he has bestowed on them.

Give each participant a small gift box and two small squares of paper. Each square of paper should have printed on it, "God's gift to me" and "My gift to God."

Play some soft music for background and ask participants to spend some time in quiet prayer and meditation. During this time, they should reflect on what sorts of gifts God has given them, and what they might be able to make of these gifts. Ask everyone to write on each square of paper one gift they have identified that God has bestowed. Then ask them to write a specific action they will take to use this gift in God's service. This could be as internal as spending more time in loving contemplation of God or as external as deciding to teach a catechism class. The type and magnitude of the use of the gift is not of importance. Both bits of paper for each participant should say the same things. One should go in the gift box and be left at the altar (or other suitable place) as an offering. The other should go home with participants and be reviewed in one month to see if the action has been taken.

Closing Prayer

Dear God, we want to praise your name and glorify you in everything we do. We recognize that sometimes we fall short of using the gifts you have given us to further your plan. We see that this especially happens when we are suffering, and we begin to question your will and your plan. Help us, dear Lord to see you in everything. Help us to know you have a plan for us, and that your loving care is always with us. Help us to use your gifts more generously, more cheerfully. We thank you for giving us such an abundance of gifts, and ask that you begin to use us more fully in whatever way you desire. Amen

Extension Activities

❖ Participants may want to continue the poetry activity that they began during the retreat. Most people will probably need more time to complete the poem satisfactorily, and some participants may wish to continuing working on this.

❖ Only a few of the scriptural verses listed are addressed in the reflection and the activities for this retreat. Participants may want to choose a different set of scriptural verses to examine. They then may want to write a reflection of their own using some or all of these verses.

❖ During their quiet reflection and journaling about the painful event in their lives, participants may have unearthed new insights or new concerns that they are now ready to examine. They might like to explore these more fully with the help of a counselor, spiritual director or wise friend. Perhaps now is the time when they are able to ask themselves what God wanted them to learn during this difficult time.

❖ For further reading, participants may be interested in reading the books mentioned in the reflection.

- J. Robert Clinton, *The Making of a Leader*
- C.S. Lewis, *The Problem of Pain*
- Philip Yancey, *Where is God When it Hurts?*

❖ Additional readings beyond these could include:

- James Fowler, *The Stages of Spiritual Growth*
- C. S. Lewis, *A Grief Observed*
- Victor Frankl, *Man's Search for Meaning*

Contemporary Poets of Prayer

Images of God

Ann Carson, "God's Justice," in *Glass, Irony and God*, New Directions Publishing Company, 1995.

Carl Dennis, "The God Who Loves You," in New *and Selected Poems: 1974-2004*, Penguin Books, 2004.

Francis X. Gaspar, "Now the Moon Is in the First Quarter, in *A Field Guide to the Heavens*, The University of Wisconsin Press, 1999.

Andrew Hudgins, "Christ as Gardner," in *The Never-Ending: New Poems*, Houghton Mifflin, 1991.

Mark Jarman, "Unholy Sonnets No. 1," in *Unholy Sonnets*, Story Line Press, 2000.

Mary Karr, "Descending Theology: The Garden," in *Sinners Welcome*, HarperCollins, 2006.

Czeslaw Milosz, "An Alcoholic Enters the Gates of Heaven," *New and Collected Poems: 1931-2001*, HarperCollins, 2003.

Pattiann Rogers, "The Possible Suffering of God," in *The Dream of the Marsh Wren*, Milkweed Editions, 1999.

God in Nature

Francis X. Gaspar, "A Field Guide to the Heavens," in *A Field Guide to the Heavens*, The University of Wisconsin Press, 2004.

Francis X. Gaspar, "I invite the Angel Gabriel, but Only the Wind Comes," in *Night of a Thousand Blossoms*, Alice James Books, 2004.

Jane Kenyon, "Let Evening Come," in *Kenyon's Collected Poems*, Graywolf Press, 2007.

Denise Levertov, "A Swan in Falling Snow," in *The Selected Poems of Denise Levertov*, New Direction Books, 2002.

Mary Oliver, "The Summer Day," in *Why I Wake Early*, Beacon Press, 2005.

Pattiann Rogers, "The Dream of the Marsh Wren," in *The Dream of the Marsh Wren*, Milkweed Editions, 1999.

Pattiann Rogers, " 'God is in the Details,' Says the Mathematician Freeman J. Dyson," in *Song of the World Becoming*, Milkweed Editions, 2001.

Luci Shaw, "The Golden Ration & the Coriolis Force," in *Water Lines*, Eerdmans, 2003.

Prayer

Scott Cairns, "The More Earnest Prayer of Christ," in *Recovered Body*, George Braziller, 1998.

Denise Levertov, "The Poetics of Faith," in *The Stream and the Sapphire: Selected Poems on Religious Themes*, New Direction Books, 1997.

Andrew Hudgins, "Praying Drunk," in *The Never-Ending: New Poems*, Houghton Mifflin Company, 1991.

Czeslaw Milosz, "Veni Creator," in *New and Collected Poems: 1931-2001*, HarperCollins, 2003.

Franz Wright, "Petition," in *God's Silence*, Alfred A. Knoph, 2006.

Spiritual Growth

Mark Jarman, "Unholy Sonnets, No. 10," in *Unholy Sonnets*, Story Line Press, 2000.

Seamus Heany, "Digging," in *Opened Ground*, Farrar, Stauss and Giroux, 1998.

Thomas Merton, "Night Flowering Cactus," in *New and Selected Poems of Thomas Merton,* New Direction Books, 1967.

Andrew Hudgins, "After Muscling through Sharp Greenery," in *Babylon in a Jar: New Poems*, Mariner Books, Houghton Mifflin Company, 1998.

Stanley Kunitz, "The Layers," in *Passing Through*, W.W. Norton, 1995.

Mary Oliver, "The Blackwater Woods," in *Why I Wake Early*, Beacon Press, 2005.

Theodore Roethke, "The Waking," *The Collected Poems of Theodore Roethke*, Anchor Books, Random House, 1991.

Authors

James Green

Jim has worked as a naval officer, deputy sheriff, high school English teacher, professor of education, and administrator in both public schools and universities. His academic publications include three books, as well as numerous monographs and articles in professional journals. His poetry has appeared in literary magazines in England, Ireland, and the USA; and a collection of his poems, *Stations of the Cross* (Finishing Line Books), was nominated by the publisher for the Modern Language Association's Conference on Christianity and Literature 2009 Book of the Year. He holds B.A. and M.S. degrees in English and Education from Missouri State University, a Ph.D. in Education from Saint Louis University, and an M.F.A. in Creative Writing from Antioch University Los Angeles.

Sheryl O'Sullivan

Sheryl has been an elementary teacher and principal and a professor of teacher education during her 40-year career. Her academic publications include five books and numerous monographs and articles in professional journals. In addition, she has published several works for children in such magazines as *Cricket*. Her doctorate is from Ball State University in early childhood education and literacy, and she holds an M.A. in Religion from Azusa Pacific University. Currently a professor of literacy at Gordon State College in Georgia, her vocation includes leading retreats organized around various themes, among them poetry as prayer.

www.ingramcontent.com/pod-product-compliance
Lightning Source LLC
Chambersburg PA
CBHW070524030426
42337CB00016B/2100